The Early Learning Goals in practice

by Liz Wilcock

Contents

Published by Practical Pre-School Books, A Division of MA Education Ltd, St Jude's Church, Dulwich Road, Herne Hill, London, SE24 0PB.

Tel: 020 7738 5454

www.practicalpreschoolbooks.com

© MA Education Ltd 2013

Design: Alison Cutler **fonthill**creative 01722 717043

All images © MA Education Ltd. All photos taken by Lucie Carlier.

ISBN 978-1-909280-26-7

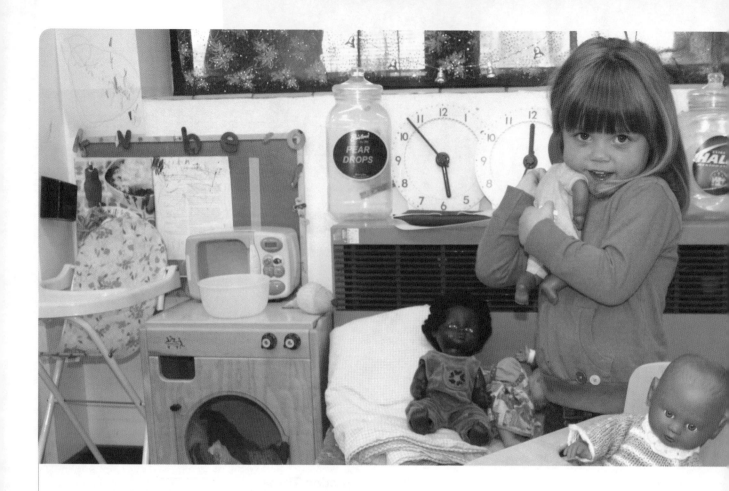

Introduction

In the Statutory Framework for the Early Years Foundation Stage book, which came into force in September 2012, the learning and development requirements are described in plain English.

These comprise of:

- the seven areas of learning and development and the educational programmes

- the early learning goals, which summarise the knowledge, skills and understanding that all young children should have gained by the end of the Reception year; and

- the assessment requirements (when and how practitioners must assess children's achievements, and when and how they should discuss children's progress with parents and/or carers).

This book has a focus on the early learning goals.

Prior to looking at each of the early learning goals, we need to understand that the areas of learning and development now fall into two categories:

- Prime Areas of Learning

- Specific Areas of Learning

In 2010, Dame Claire Tickell, Chief Executive of Action for Children, carried out an independent review of the EYFS – her remit was to see how the Framework could be less bureaucratic and more focused on supporting children's early learning.

In *The Early Years: Foundations for Life, Health and Learning*, Dame Claire Tickell explains her reasons for introducing prime and specific areas of learning into the Framework:

> *'Evidence shows that personal, social and emotional development, communication and language and*

physical development are essential foundations for children's life, learning and success. Therefore, I am recommending these are identified as prime areas of learning in the EYFS. Sitting alongside these, I am proposing that literacy, mathematics, understanding of the world, and expressive arts and design are identified as the specific areas of learning in which these prime skills are applied. I believe this model for the areas of learning is clear, unambiguous, and simple and should help all early years practitioners to understand better how to support children's development.

Many practitioners told me that they would like to see the early learning goals – which define the level of development most children should have reached by the end of the year in which they turn 5 – reduced and simplified, and made more sensitive to the needs of summer born children and to those children who are fast developers. To address this, I recommend that the early learning goals are reduced in number from 69 to 17. I also recommend that for each goal, a simple three-part scale is established which sets out what working towards, what achieving, and what exceeding each goal looks like. Many people spoke to me about tensions with the current formal assessment of children's level of development at age 5 – the EYFS Profile. In consequence, I am recommending this is radically simplified, and reduced in size from 117 pieces of information to 20 pieces of information that capture a child's level of development in a much less burdensome way'.

As a result, the areas of learning and development and their aspects are now presented as in the table opposite.

In Section One of this book, we will consider the **aspects of the prime areas of learning**.

In Section Two, we will consider the **aspects of the specific areas of learning**. The table shows the aspects we will be focusing on.

In Section Three, we will consider the **EYFS Profile**.

Area of Learning	Aspects
Prime Areas	
Communication and Language	Listening and attention
	Understanding
	Speaking
Physical Development	Moving and handling
	Health and self-care
Personal, Social and Emotional Development	Making relationships
	Self-confidence and self-awareness
	Managing feelings and behaviour
Specific Areas	
Literacy	Reading
	Writing
Mathematics	Numbers
	Shape, space and measure
Understanding the World	People and communities
	The world
	Technology
Expressive Arts and Design	Exploring and using media and materials
	Being imaginative

Information for this book was sourced from:

- *The Early Years: Foundations for Life, Health and Learning* (2011)

- The Statutory Framework (2012)

- Development Matters (2012 non statutory guidance)

- Ofsted (www.ofsted.gov.uk)

- Department for Education (www.education.gov.uk)

Section One: The prime areas are at the heart of each child's learning

From birth, babies begin to develop quickly in response to relationships and experiences. The prime areas continue to be at the core of learning throughout the EYFS – they run through and support learning in all other areas.

Let's look at each one in turn.

Communication and Language

This is all about developing children's listening and attention skills, helping children's understanding of language and developing their speaking skills. Early language development is crucial for future learning and school readiness.

Early Learning Goals

Listening and attention

Children listen attentively in a range of situations. They listen to stories, accurately anticipating key events and respond to what they hear with relevant comments, questions or actions. They give their attention to what others say and respond appropriately, while engaged in another activity.

Understanding

Children follow instructions involving several ideas or actions. They answer 'how' and 'why' questions about their experiences and in response to stories or events.

Speaking

Children express themselves effectively, showing awareness of listeners' needs. They use past, present and future forms accurately when talking about events that have happened or are to happen in the future. They develop their own narratives and explanations by connecting ideas or events.

In terms of **listening and attention**, let's look at how you can:

1. Provide opportunities for children to listen attentively.

2. Encourage children to listen to stories, accurately anticipating key events and respond to what they hear with relevant comments, questions or actions.

3. Help children to give their attention to what is being said to them and respond appropriately, whilst still being involved in an activity.

Opportunities to listen attentively

Teachers at John Rankin Infant and Nursery School provide plenty of opportunities for children to listen attentively in the Foundation Stage One setting, as part of a whole class, in small groups and independently throughout the session.

Each day the children are expected to take part in whole class input sessions. When the children first join the class, these sessions are very short and might be as simple as listening for their name in the register and giving a gesture to show they have heard, or answer "good morning" if they are feeling confident enough. 'As the children become more accustomed to sitting and listening we begin to extend this time and include identifying the days of the week and the weather. Eventually we will begin to use this time to read a key text, do a number activity or introduce some art or investigation work that we want the children to participate in that day. There is lots of opportunity during these whole class inputs for the children to ask and answer questions and we try to make them as active as possible. For example, if we are learning to use the language of number through songs and rhymes we will provide props for the children to use such as 5 flying saucers sown onto gloves'.

During whole class inputs children are expected to be "Super Sitters". Teachers display a picture of what a super sitter looks like, with legs crossed, hands in laps and sitting up straight. Teachers explain to the children that sitting like this will help them to concentrate as they won't be distracted by having something in their hands to fiddle with or having someone else touching them. Children are constantly praised for their good sitting and the class toy, Super Sitting Kitten, chooses a new Super Sitter each day to sit with during the input session.

Open forums and rounds during circle time session also encourage the children to listen attentively. During an open forum the children are asked to contribute to a certain topic of conversation. For example, how can we keep the Nursery a safe and happy place? They need to listen to what other children are saying in order to contribute effectively to the conversation. During a round the children wait to hold the special toy that is being passed around the circle before they speak. They sit quietly while they are waiting and listen to what the other children are saying.

Much of early phonics teaching is also dedicated to teaching the children how to listen. Teachers play a range of listening games with the children and a particular favourite is to fill a box with items that make different sounds and ask the children to guess what is making the sound. Children play matching games with instruments – they love to make sound tents by placing fabric over tables. Teachers hide a selection of instruments inside the tent with matching instruments outside. Someone goes inside the tent to play an instrument and the children on the outside have to guess what instrument is being played just by listening to the sound. Teachers also encourage children to listen to similarities in sounds that words make. Teachers also regularly make collections of objects that begin with the same letter sound or that rhyme with each other.

Whenever playing outside the children are encouraged to listen to sounds around them and record them when they can. Teachers often take the children on listening walks around the grounds and provide opportunities for children to explore sounds through activities such as Outdoor Drums. Adults talk regularly to the children about the sounds they are making and how they compare to other sounds.

Stories

The book area is a small, cosy and communication friendly space that not only has a range of books for the children to look at but also a selection of cushions and blankets for the children to snuggle up in. It is covered with fabric to give a den like feel, which provides the children with a sense of privacy. Children can often be found in our book area sharing stories with each other. They will look at the pictures and create their own narratives and they usually have a group of friends sitting around them listening. They love to pretend to be the teacher and sit and listen to each other attentively. Audio books can also be found in the book area. Children are able to self select the story they would like to listen to and play it on the CD player. The children enjoy this because they can use technology to hear their favourite tales.

'We have a designated storytime every day as well as sharing key texts for our themes every week. When we read a story we try to encourage the children to contribute as much as possible. In order to achieve

this we try not to ask too many questions, especially questions that only have one answer! Instead we will comment on the story and allow children time to add their own comments without always having to put their hand up. For example we might start a comment with "I wonder why…" We find children are more likely to contribute to a shared read like this than if they are put on the spot with lots of questions that only have a right or wrong answer'.

Whenever teachers do need to ask children a question about a book, they follow the ten second rule, which means they give the children ten seconds to think about the question before expecting them to answer it.

Giving attention to what is said to them

Teachers always plan from the children's interests in the setting and are constantly supplementing learning bays with resources that will capture the children's imagination. As children explore these resources, adults may play alongside them, commenting and modelling language. For example if a child is using the Dino World an adult might share their knowledge of dinosaurs or talk about a visit to the Natural History Museum. The children then feel encouraged to share their own knowledge but they do not need to stop what they are doing to show the adult what they know about dinosaurs.

In terms of **understanding**, let's look at how you can:

1. Support children to follow instructions involving several ideas or actions.

2. Provide opportunities for children to answer 'how' and 'why' questions about their experiences and in response to stories or events.

Following instructions

The simplest way teachers at John Rankin Infant and Nursery School support children with following instructions, is through daily routine. At tidy up time each child is given a specific job to do as part of a group, such as tidying the role-play area. The children are told what is expected of them and the task is made easier with resource drawers being clearly labelled so the children know where to put things away.

Each child has a pair of indoor shoes and a pair of outdoor shoes at Nursery. Teachers encourage independence and teach children to change these by themselves. The adult gives simple instructions for the children to follow and will model what to do when necessary. Once children can change their own shoes they are expected to put their other shoes away in the basket. Instructions are also given for putting coats and other outdoor clothing on. The children also follow simple instructions when getting changed for a PE session, and of course help is given when needed.

Also, in PE sessions children learn to follow simple instructions to play a game. Parachute games are very popular in the Nursery and the children certainly follow instructions more efficiently if they are doing something they enjoy. They soon realise the game works better if they all work together and follow the instructions.

Staff also value the idea of learning for a purpose and making sure the children have a quality outcome at the end of a task. When it comes to following instructions teachers have found that a great way to approach this is to make recipe books with the children. For example, the children can cut out pictures that show instructions for making a sandwich and then stick them in the correct order in their own stapled books. Once the children have a set of picture instructions to follow we provide the ingredients at the snack table and the children are able to make their own sandwiches, giving their recipe books a true purpose.

Answering 'how' and 'why' questions

'At the end of each session we have a Reflection Time, when we ask the children which learning bays they have visited that day and what they learnt there. If they have been exploring capacity in the water tray we might ask them how they found out how many cups of water filled the jug and why the jug of water did not fill up the ice cream tub. We might relate a story like this to Mr Archimedes' Bath and talk to the children about why they think the water spilt out of the bath and how Mr Archimedes' could keep the water in the bath'.

On the spot reflection is also important with young children as not all children will have the confidence to share their learning with the whole class. Adult focus

learning opportunities are planned every day and as adults work with the children they constantly encourage them to reflect. For example, when mixing colours at the art table an adult might ask the children how they could make a different colour such as green or why they think the dark blue has got lighter when they added white.

Teachers also find the junk modelling or construction area are great places to encourage the understanding of how and why questions. Staff like the children to plan the models they are going to make before they make them. They provide design sheets for children to draw their model on. The adult asks children which materials they are going to use and why, and also asks them how they are going to fix their materials together to achieve their final creation. Once the children have made a model the adult might ask them what they like about their model and what they feel went well as they were making it. The adult might also ask them what they might do to improve their model if the had more time. Why have they chosen to improve that part of the model and how will they do it?

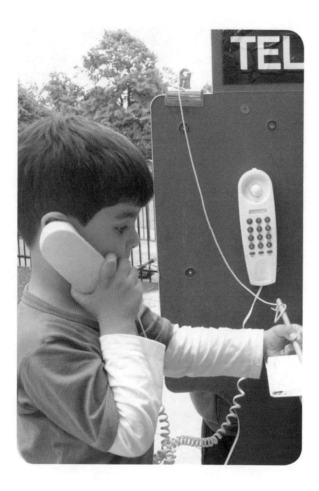

In terms of **speaking**, let's look at how you can:

1. Support children to express themselves effectively.

2. Encourage children to use past, present and future tenses accurately when talking about events that have happened or are to happen in the future.

3. Provide opportunities for children to develop their own narratives and explanations by connecting ideas or events.

Express themselves effectively

There are a number of ways in which children can be supported to verbally express themselves – although for some children, this can be a real challenge. For children to effectively express themselves, they need time to develop confidence to speak – some children may speak with ease to an adult on a one-one basis, but may struggle to speak out in a small group, even if they have the vocabulary. The role of the adult is to encourage children to communicate their thoughts, ideas and feelings through a variety of ways, such as through song and dance, art as well as verbally.

Show and tell is one way in which children can learn to express themselves, supported by attentive adults. When children are excited or interested in something, they will be more likely to want to share this with others – this may be to show a photograph of a new baby in their family, to talk about a memorable holiday, or just to share something that is of current interest. The child is learning to speak with confidence in a safe environment, as well as learning to listen, as others share their own news/item. Children learn how to respond to questions when adults support them to use descriptive language. The adult can help children by asking How? Why? What? Where? Who? and even encouraging other children to ask questions too.

Encouraging children to have a 'talk partner' or 'response partner' is another way to support children to become effective in their verbal expressions. Children can talk to each other about, for example, what their ideal pet would be, and why!

Role play gives children rich opportunities to express themselves – they can communicate using appropriate language for the play they are engaged in such as when they are 'in charge' giving out instructions or negotiating with others to achieve an outcome. Most practitioners consider the home corner as the area for role play, but the whole setting can be used – change your role-play area regularly to ensure it is related to any theme, which in turn, is related to the children's interests and experiences.

Using past, present and future tenses accurately

For children to comprehend the tenses i.e. past tense – the event has already happened, present tense – the event is happening now and future tense – the event is going to happen, adults need to make situations real and support children in recall as well as thinking about the future. Words such as yesterday, tomorrow, next week, this morning, tonight and last year all help children put the tenses into context when e.g. planning ahead for a party, talking about what happened previously or what is happening now. At the end of a session, children can be encouraged to reflect on what they have learnt today – which learning bays they have visited and what did they learn there?

Think about planning and preparing for a birthday party for a Teddy. Talk about how old Teddy would be, what he would need to celebrate his birthday and what presents you and the children could prepare for him. Count down the days until Teddy's birthday as you make cakes, print wrapping paper and make him birthday cards. Use language such as "Tomorrow when it's Teddy's birthday we will play party games". After the party, talk about what you and the children have done, for example "Yesterday at Teddy's party we ate cake".

Connecting ideas or events to create their own narratives and explanations

To support children to connect their thoughts and ideas, staff plan for experiments or construction activities that follow a structure of four simple steps.

1. "What do we know about…?": 'We would begin by asking the children what they know about a particular theme. For example after a visit from the fire brigade we might introduce them to a fictional fireman and tell them that we are going to design and make some emergency fire-fighting vehicles for him to use. We would create a thought shower of ideas with the children of all the different fire-fighting vehicles they know of. All children's contributions are valued and recorded on the board'.

2. "How could we…?: 'Next we would choose a popular choice from the thought shower as an example. We would ask the children how they will make this model. What construction materials might they use? How will they fix the materials together? What tools will they need? What do they want their final product to look like? From this discussion we would demonstrate drawing a design for the fire vehicle'.

3. "Let's do it!": 'The children will go to the construction area to design and build their models. This part of the process will be supported but not guided by adults. It should be the children's work and they need to learn from their own mistakes in order to access the next step'.

4. "What have we learnt?": 'The final step is an opportunity for children to share their work with the class. They talk about what they found easy and what they found difficult when making their model. They are then asked to think about what they could do to further improve their model in the following session'.

Staff find that this approach encourages children to talk freely about the theme, sharing their ideas and connecting their thoughts, e.g. "If the glue doesn't hold the boxes together what could I use instead?"

Physical Development

This is all about helping children to be able to move around and be able to handle things. It is also about helping children to understand about health and their own self care.

Early Learning Goals

Moving and handling
Children show good control and co-ordination in large and small movements. They move confidently in a range of ways, safely negotiating space. They handle equipment and tools effectively, including pencils for writing.

Health and self-care
Children know the importance of physical exercise and a healthy diet for good health, and talk about ways to keep healthy and safe. They manage their own basic hygiene and personal needs successfully, including dressing and going to the toilet independently.

In terms of **moving and handling**, let's look at how you can:

1. Guide children in gaining good control in large and small movements.

2. Provide children with opportunities to move confidently in a range of ways, safely negotiating space.

3. Support children to handle equipment and tools effectively, including pencils for writing.

Children who attend John Rankin Infant and Nursery School have full access to a large garden – children have a regular weekly PE slot in the hall and the use of a large field space, where staff take the children to in all weathers, throughout the year. Each space is a different size and has different physical obstacles for the children to overcome, for example, the field has a Secret Garden attached to it where the children have to duck and weave around the trees and plants. Having a range of indoor and outdoor spaces for the children to explore helps them build up confidence and control to move in different ways, adapting their movements accordingly. For instance, they soon learn that it is not so easy to run around the Nursery classroom as it is to run around the school field. This also helps them to develop a sense of safety and to think about the importance of keeping themselves safe.

Control in large and small scale movements

To support the children with making controlled movements, staff provide a range of daily tasks that may include pushing and pulling games, such as Row the Boat, carrying heavy items, for example small buckets of sand or water, and stretching and reaching activities such as using

pulleys to lift items in the construction area of the patio. The children have access to trikes and scooters that they ride around a wiggly track and wheelbarrows and digging equipment in the garden. Children are encouraged during tidy up time to use wet cloths to wipe paint from the tables or board rubbers to clean the whiteboard. They also have regular access to the interactive whiteboard, where they have to use controlled smaller scale movements to drag and drop items around the screen.

Children often play games such as Follow the Leader, which is a great game to link to other areas of learning! Staff and children often play it during phonics sessions when the children are copying body percussion sounds, which are sounds that can be made with the body, such as clapping hands, stamping feet, clicking fingers. It can be played indoors and outdoors and of course can be linked to stories, such as The Pied Piper. The children love playing this game and build their own confidence in leading the line and practising different ways of moving.

In the garden there is an adventure trail climbing frame, which consists of a balance beam, wobbly bridge and stepping stones. Teachers set the children challenges on the climbing frame, for example "Can you get across the bridge without holding onto the railings?". They also provide other physical challenges in the garden in the form of obstacle courses or "Mini Olympics" style learning opportunities. After reading a story about a race staff might challenge the children to race each other around the obstacle course, time each other as they complete the Mini-Olympics activities or take part in racing and chasing games, such as egg and spoon racing or Stuck in the Mud.

Children always love playing throwing, rolling, fetching and receiving games, but first need to learn how to throw and catch a large ball. Staff teach skills like this through specific PE sessions in the school hall and then provide opportunities for the children to practise independently in the garden throughout the week. Games such as Piggy in the Middle not only help the children consolidate these skills but also promote team work. Parachute games are also great for this. The nursery has a large parachute that can fit all 30 of our morning nursery children plus adults around the edge. Teachers use the parachute to help practise control of equipment such as a ball. For example, the children love to play Popcorn where a member of staff places a number of light balls onto the parachute and everyone works together to lift the parachute up and down in order to bounce the balls off. The children also love working together to roll a larger ball around the top of the parachute. The aim of the game here is to keep the ball on the parachute and not let it fall off the edge!

Moving confidently in a range of ways

Young children love listening to music, especially familiar music such as Nursery Rhymes or children's television theme tunes. Music is played regularly and the children enjoy dancing to it and playing the musical instruments along to the beat and rhythm. For the smaller afternoon nursery class, where the children are very young, staff often have soothing classical music playing as the children enter. This has a very calming effect on the children and in response their body movements tend to be a lot calmer and relaxed without them even realising.

During certain themes staff also play music from different cultures. For example, during the theme of Chinese New Year, staff would play Chinese music each day in the music area and encourage children to move imaginatively to it. Staff would then show them video clips of a Chinese Dragon dancing and encourage them to work together to create a dancing dragon. Children also have access to a range of instruments so that they can play along to the music. Some of the children once made a Chinese Dragon costume, which staff make use of every year! The children love taking it in turns to be the head and following each other around in a Chinese Dragon dance.

The PE sessions and garden also provide children with opportunities to practise their slithering, shuffling, rolling, crawling, walking, running, jumping, skipping, sliding and hopping. Inside, teachers provide large wooden blocks and planks, which the children often use to build their own balance beams and obstacle courses in the construction area. During an independent activity like this the children are practising carrying equipment carefully and safely, as well as their gross motor skills.

Handling equipment and tools effectively

As the children's gross motor skills develop they become more able to use their fine motor to manipulate tools such as scissors, paintbrushes, pens and pencils.

Teachers often find that young children love to cut paper with scissors. To help focus this interest and develop their scissor control, staff supplement the writing area with cutting and sticking activities such as cutting out paper clothes to dress the cardboard bear. This is a wonderful way to link their love of cutting to what the weather is doing outside as the children need to decide which clothes Bear needs to wear that day.

Children also have the opportunity to use a range of tools in junk modelling area. This might be to make their own musical instruments. During such an activity the children will need to use their scissor skills to cut tape or develop other fine motor skills to attach split pins or staples. They will also need to use controlled movements to pour resources such as seeds into the instrument they are making.

To encourage the children to begin making recognisable marks on paper, staff regularly promote finger painting at the art or malleable table. They display handwriting patterns, such as zig zags, for the children to copy and encourage them to draw lines and circles on their paper. They also link finger painting activities to Expressive Arts and Design by supporting the children to enclose spaces to represent objects as they paint.

Manipulations tasks such as rolling, stretching and squeezing playdough are also planned for and staff often provide playdough mats and cutters that are related to the theme in order to spark children's interests.

In terms of **health and self care**, let's look at how you can:

1. Guide children to understand the importance of good health (physical exercise and a healthy diet) and support them to talk about ways to keep healthy and safe.

2. Support children to manage their own basic hygiene and personal needs successfully, including dressing and going to the toilet independently.

Understanding the importance of good health

In the Nursery setting, children are encouraged each day to make healthy choices about the food they eat. Fruit is provided at the snack table and the children self select the fruit they would like to eat. There is always a choice of either milk or water at the snack table and many of the children also bring their own water bottle to Nursery, which they can access easily whenever they want a drink. Keeping hydrated helps keep children alert and ready to learn new things.

Children who stay for lunch are encouraged to either bring healthy lunchboxes or choose from a menu of freshly cooked healthy food from the school lunch menu. Staff talk regularly to the children about the choices they make at the snack table and talk about the importance of eating a range of healthy foods.

On occasion, staff will also supplement food at the snack table. For example during a Chinese New Year theme staff will provide a selection of Chinese food and talk to the children about Chinese takeaway. Children love to share their experiences of such food and staff always make sure the children are aware that a takeaway can be a nice treat but would be unhealthy to eat too often.

Young children often get tired, even during a three hour session. Nurseries can be busy places and it is very easy for children to become over stimulated. Teachers often find the younger children in the afternoon nursery become very tired during their session. One way staff have overcome this is to create cosy, comfortable areas that the children know are quiet areas of learning. The book area is small and covered with fabric. Inside the book area, there are blankets and cushions and the children know that if they are feeling tired, they can go for a rest in there. Staff also provide cushions in other parts of the room to help break up the large and mainly wooden room. Little baskets of books are placed near these cushions to provide more quiet areas where children can relax.

Staff also encourage children to take responsibility for the clothes and shoes that they wear. For example, when planning to go on a walk, staff would ask the children to assess the weather and what clothes they will need to put on. They remind the children of previous walks, such as when they went to the field, and ask them to think about what the ground was like under foot and assess whether they think they will need wellies and waterproof trousers this time.

Teachers always begin the weekly PE sessions with a warm up game which is active and fun. After the game, staff encourage children to think about the changes that are happening to their bodies. They feel their heartbeats to see if their heart is beating faster, they listen to their breathing and if the children feel their bodies have warmed up they are encourage to take off their jumpers. Conversations like this happen regularly and the children soon get used to assessing the changes that have happened to their bodies and whether they have done enough warm up exercise.

Managing hygiene and personal needs

After the children have been taught how to use the snack table, the use of it is completely independent. The children are expected to wash their own hands before they have their snack and you soon get to know which children you need to monitor! When children first start, Nursery staff teach them how to wash their hands properly and sing the song "This is the way we wash our hands…" (to the tune of Here we go round the Mulberry

Bush). Sometimes staff ask the school nurse to come in and show the children under ultra violet light where they have left germs on their hands.

As much as possible, staff expect children to change into their own PE kits. Children need to take off their school clothes and change into shorts and T-shirt. After PE sessions they need to change back again. Changing into PE kits each PE session teaches the children that it is important to wear different clothes for exercise. Staff talk to the children about the fact that they get hot when they do PE and this can make their clothes dirty and sometimes smelly. Staff encourage children who are struggling with self help skills by giving them a small step to complete. For example, a member of staff might help a child take their arms out of a T-shirt and then ask them to pull it off over their heads.

Increasingly, staff are finding that they are supporting children with potty or toilet training when they enter Foundation Stage One. They are fortunate to have toilets of different heights, including one very low toilet that is easy for the children to get on and off. Staff provide toilet trainer seats and low level steps to aid children with the use of the toilet and there are potties for those who need them. Staff also discuss with the parents what they are doing at home with regards to toilet training and try to support children in the same way in Nursery.

Personal, Social and Emotional Development

This is all about developing children's self-confidence and self-esteem, that is, how children feel about themselves. It is also about helping children to manage their feelings and their behaviour, and supporting children to make relationships with others and to understand others too.

Early Learning Goals

Making relationships

Children play co-operatively, taking turns with others. They take account of one another's ideas about how to organise their activity. They show sensitivity to others' needs and feelings, and form positive relationships with adults and other children.

Self-confidence and self-awareness

Children are confident to try new activities, and say why they like some activities more than others. They are confident to speak in a familiar group, will talk about their ideas, and will choose the resources they need for their chosen activities. They say when they do or don't need help.

Managing feelings and behaviour

Children talk about how they and others show feelings, talk about their own and others' behaviour, and its consequences, and know that some behaviour is unacceptable. They work as part of a group or class, and understand and follow the rules. They adjust their behaviour to different situations, and take changes of routine in their stride.

In terms of **making relationships**, let's look at how you can:

1. Encourage children to play co-operatively, and take turns when playing.

2. Support children to take account of one another's ideas about how to organise their activities.

3. Encourage children to show sensitivity to the needs and feelings of others and form positive relationships with adults and other children in the setting.

Teachers at John Rankin Infant and Nursery School find that children need a lot of support in this area when they first enter Foundation One. Many of the children have spent the first three years of life at home with maybe a sibling for company and find entering a large and busy environment containing lots of children quite daunting at first.

If the children don't already have a friend in the Nursery, they need support in making friendships with children they don't know.

They also need to form good relationships with the adults in the setting so that they trust the adults and want to work with them as they demonstrate some of the key elements above.

Playing co-operatively

On a daily basis, the teachers provide children with a range of toys, games and learning opportunities that encourage them to work together. They try as much as possible to take the children's interests into account when planning these activities so that the children want to come in and play. The large floor space allows plenty of opportunity for children to build a train track together and share out the trains equally between them. Similarly they can work together to use wooden bricks to build a garage for the cars or a farm for the animals.

Familiar stories such as The Three Little Pigs can encourage children to work together to build a house from large foam bricks. As the children become more familiar with each other and form stronger friendships, teachers set challenges for them, such as working with a partner to make a bug pot for a bug hunt. The adults will get down on the floor and work with the children, demonstrating how to share resources and wait for their turn.

Puzzles and games are a great way to encourage children to work together and take turns. There is a designated puzzle area within the setting where a whole host of puzzles, board games and card games are kept. The children have daily access to these resources and are able to move them to other areas if they need to. For example they might prefer to move a floor puzzle to the large open floor space, or a pairs game to the quiet book area. Again, the adults will join the children at these activities when they can and take part in the game themselves. Children are expected to wait for their turn as they play the game and taught to go round in a circle so that no player is left out. When completing puzzles an adult might say "Let's find all the bits that make the elephant part of the picture first" and encourage the children to work together on one part of the puzzle at a time. Similarly, group games are encouraged in the garden where the children are supported to work together and play parachute games or practise their throwing and catching skills with the large balls.

Taking into account one another's ideas

At the beginning of a new theme, teachers always ask children what they already know. This is done through small group and whole class discussions and often follows a story stimulus or an opportunity to explore a relevant object. The children are encouraged to listen to each other and extend on their ideas if they can. For example, after reading 'After the Storm' to the children, the adults introduced them to a cuddly toy rabbit which was soaking wet. The children were asked how they could keep the rabbit dry if there was another storm. What did they know about keeping dry in the rain? How could we find out which materials would keep Rabbit dry? Together, the children planned an experiment to test materials in the water tray and concluded as a class what they would make for Rabbit and which material they would use. In this process the children were listening to each other, sharing their findings and making a decision about how an activity would progress as a class.

Forming positive relationships

Something that the teachers have found very effective when it comes to forming positive relationships within the setting is to identify and celebrate all the things that make all the children special as individuals. There is a Gallery wall in the setting which can display anything, from a piece of work the children have completed in the setting, to photographs or items they have brought in from home. Whenever the teachers introduce a new theme, they ask children if they have anything at home that might contribute to the theme, for example, a photo of their pets or shells from the beach. Adults are encouraged to add to the Gallery too so that the children can see there are many similarities and differences between not only themselves but also the adults.

Adults are the greatest role-models when it comes to forming relationships. On a daily basis the children see the adults in the setting being welcoming, kind and sensitive to each other and the children. They have time to listen to the children's interests and talk to them about their weekends or home life. The children see the adults behaving this way and join in too!

In terms of **self-confidence and self-awareness**, let's look at how you can:

1. Give children confidence to try out new activities and be able to say why they prefer some activities to others.

2. Provide opportunities for children to talk about their ideas, and choose their resources they need in order to plan and carry out chosen activities.

3. Encourage children to say when they do or do not need help.

Teachers at John Rankin Infant and Nursery School help children to develop self confidence by allowing them to make informed choices about their own learning. The school has a planning board displayed in the carpet area, which has four choices of learning opportunity related to our theme. These opportunities run alongside any adult focus tasks that the children might be taking part in, and of course the children are still able to access their own choice of resources. Teachers discuss these tasks with the children at the beginning of each session and at the end of the session; children are invited to share what they have been learning in those areas.

Confidence to try new activities

Learning opportunities within the setting are constantly supplemented by the activities planned for on the Planning Board. These extra theme-related activities are available for 1-2 weeks. Teachers try not to plan for the same area of learning each time as they want children to experience a range of opportunities in order to make informed decisions on what their preferred activities are. Teachers always discuss what is available in the four chosen areas before the children go to them and if necessary an adult will be on hand to demonstrate how a certain resource could be used. Teachers support the children to access these resources independently so that they can build their own confidence in exploring and investigating without the presence of an adult. The investigation area is a great place to develop the children's self confidence. For example children are often happy to spend extended periods of time watching toy animals melt out of blocks of ice and talk about how and why the ice is changing. They can then share this information with the whole class at the end of the session.

Providing opportunities for children to talk

Often children will all talk at once when they are excited about an activity and find it hard to take on board other children's ideas and opinions. Teachers try to encourage our children to plan as much as possible what they are going to do before they go about doing it.

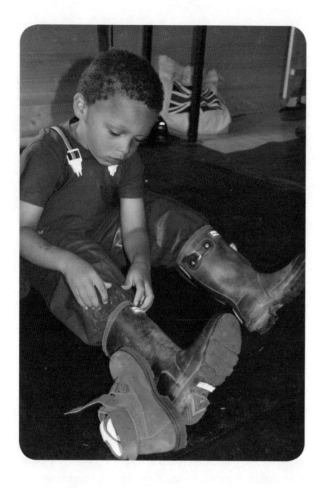

As an example, during a theme about 'pets', the role-play area was used as a vets. Children who had chosen to play in the vets that day were then encouraged to discuss beforehand what they might do. Teachers will support the children to decide the roles they might take in the vets and what that might entail. For example, if you choose to be the receptionist then your jobs would be to write bookings in the diary, answer the phone and take payment from customers. As children get more used to this format for discussion they become much more efficient at organising their own play and in turn far more independent.

Encouraging children to say when they do or do not need help

A free flow snack table in the setting can be accessed by the children throughout the session. The children are taught to self register at the snack table, wash their hands independently and choose their own fruit and drink. The children do not have adult support at the snack table unless they ask for it. The children enjoy this freedom and being trusted to make sensible

decisions about their own health and well being. If the children encounter a problem, such as not being able to open their banana, they will usually ask another child to help before approaching an adult. Teachers find this helps the children to develop their own problem solving skills and ask themselves "Can I do this on my own?". The children then learn to transfer these skills to other problems they may encounter around the Nursery, such as "What should I do if all the pencils are blunt?".

In terms of **managing feelings and behaviour**, let's look at ways in which you can:

1. Encourage children to talk about how they and others show feelings and manage their own feelings.

2. Encourage children to talk about their own and others' behaviour and its consequences.

3. Support children to work together as part of a group or class and understand and follow the rules. How can you support children to adjust their behaviour to different situations and to changes in routine?

Feelings

Talking about feelings can be very difficult for a young child as they often don't understand how they feel. Teachers at John Rankin Infant and Nursery School spend a lot of time in the setting looking at pictures of different facial expressions and practising making them. They sing 'If You're Happy and You Know It' regularly and talk about why we are feeling happy. Sometimes teachers will change the words to 'If You're Grumpy and You Know It', or 'If You're Sad...'.

At least once a week teachers conduct a PSED Circle Time, usually in small groups, and provide opportunities for children to talk about feelings in an open forum. Often a puppet is experiencing a certain feeling, such as anger, and the children suggest ways to help him calm down and feel better. We try to relate the puppet's issues with something that has arisen in the setting, such as feeling angry because another puppet has knocked down their tower. Children are regularly asked questions such as "How would you feel if...?" and are encouraged to use a range of vocabulary to describe feelings.

Behaviour

The setting follows Jenny Moseley's Golden Rules of 'Do be Gentle, Do be Kind'. When the children first enter the setting, they create their own handprint to add to the Golden Rules board. The children are told that by adding their handprint they are expected to follow the Golden Rules. Their names and photos are clearly displayed with their handprints so the children can easily identify themselves if the adult ever needs to refer them to the rules they have agreed to.

Puppets are used to demonstrate unwanted behaviour in the setting and children are encouraged to teach the puppets how to behave properly. Children take turns in conversation by waiting for their turn to hold the special toy before they speak.

Children are photographed using resources sensibly in the setting and these photos are displayed as prompts for all children to use. If children are not behaving as expected, teachers would stop them and ask them to look at these photos. Teachers will ask them to identify how the children in the picture are using the resources in that area, and suggest that they try to use the resources in a similar way. This encourages children to change their behaviour and take responsibility for their own learning, rather than being told "no" by an adult.

Working together to understand and follow the rules

Teachers strive to create a supportive and positive environment where all children feel valued. They ask children not to speak in a negative way about each other but to "tell us a good tale" instead. Children like to share with the adults what they have liked about another child's behaviour that day and we celebrate this with thumbs up or class claps to show each child that we are proud of them for following the rules. Each week teachers plan for a key PSED skill and ask the children to help them be detectives and spot someone who is demonstrating this skill. This might be a child who is sharing fairly or helping others in some way.

Teachers like to provide enriching learning opportunities for the children, such as visits from the fire brigade or nature walks in the extensive school grounds. Teachers

manage the children's reaction to these changes to routine by displaying a visual timetable each day. "We all look at the timetable together to remind the children what each picture means.

When there is a new picture on the timetable, we discuss it with the children and prepare them for what will happen. As a task is completed it is removed from the timetable so the children can see when the change will happen. Knowing when a change to routine will happen helps the children to manage any feelings of anxiety and prepare themselves to demonstrate the same behaviours that are usually expected in our setting".

Section Two:
The specific areas

The specific areas include essential skills and knowledge for children to participate successfully in society

The specific areas build on early development and learning beyond the prime areas. These are dependent on the prime areas – so it is not a case of the 'prime areas first and the specific areas to follow' All seven areas of learning and development are important and inter-connected. Let's look at each one in turn.

Literacy

This is all about encouraging children to link sounds and letters and to begin to read and write. Giving children access to a wide range of reading materials (books, poems, and other written materials) ignites their interest.

Early Learning Goals

Reading

Children read and understand simple sentences. They use phonic knowledge to decode regular words and read them aloud accurately. They also read some common irregular words. They demonstrate understanding when talking with others about what they have read.

Writing

Children use their phonic knowledge to write words in ways which match their spoken sounds. They also write some irregular common words. They write simple sentences which can be read by themselves and others. Some words are spelt correctly and others are phonetically plausible.

In terms of **reading**, let's look at how you can:

1. Support children to start to read and understand simple sentences.

2. Introduce phonics to assist children in decoding regular words.

3. Provide opportunities for children to talk to others about what they have read.

Victoria Park Nursery School provides younger children with a range of opportunities to make their first experiences of written words positive, mainly through books. As we know, young children, in their day to day lives, come across words that are examples of 'environmental print' such as 'Tesco' 'car park' 'exit' etc. They begin to understand that these written words are telling us, for example, that we have arrived at the supermarket. Staff at the nursery school ensure that children also hear familiar words regularly and see them written too, to help them to start making connections. Children can self register at Welcome Time by the use of name cards. Staff provide children with a wide range of activities and experiences to support their early interest in reading and writing, such as:

- Singing sessions (including speaking rhymes)

- Talking with others (peer group or adults)

- Dressing up

- Making up own stories using resources such as puppets

- Sharing books, or looking at books alone.

Repetition is a key factor in children's understanding. Staff look at and read lots of books with repetitive refrains, for example 'The Three Little Pigs', 'The Gingerbread Man'. Hearing the same story over and over again consolidates children's learning, and this is important for the children's development in reading and writing. Children in the nursery school have access to a wide range of books to choose from, such as poetry, fiction, non-fiction and wordless in the library area and throughout the play areas. Staff help children to understand that reading on each page begins at the top of the page, and reads from left to right. Children enjoy making their own books too.

Parental involvement is crucial in supporting children's reading and writing skills. The child's spoken words (and listening skills) are the very foundations for reading and writing. When parents involve their children in everyday home 'tasks' they will be helping their children to understand that the way language is put together into sentences is for a reason, that is, the way in which we communicate with each other. Encourage parents to talk to their children about what they are doing, to offer explanations and to give them time to ask questions too.

Making sounds

From an early age, children learn to make sounds that represent something, for example, when an adult asks "What does the cow say?", the child is encouraged to say "Moo". As a result, the young child connects your word (cow) to their sound (moo).

It is the development of sounds in speech that helps children with their reading. These different sounds (phonemes) combined with letters (graphemes) make up the spoken word.

This means that children can begin to understand how letters link to sounds – and this is what phonics is all about. Initially, children begin to understand that letters form words such as d-o-g = dog. Blending letters (separate sounds) in this way is a crucial skill needed for reading.

It is also important for children to hear the separate sounds in words, such as sh-ee-p. The sh sound combined with the ee sound and ending with the p letter forms the word SHEEP. Of course, the English language is not that straightforward and eventually children will need to learn about the more complicated words that just need to be learned, as they are not easily explained! An early example of this is the word 'the'.

Let's look at how the Letters and Sounds scheme can help children develop their reading skills.

Using everyday known objects, such as a cup, car, spoon and a peg, helps children to verbally spell out the sounds to form words, breaking them down into the sounds of the words, that is, c-u-p, c-a-r, sp-oo-n, p-e-g. Find these words written in books, or make your own

Victoria Park Nursery School provides children with a wide variety of ways to make marks, to develop their emergent writing skills. Staff can regularly be seen to be writing in front of the children so they can see this as a natural thing to do. If children see that writing has a purpose, such as the writing of an address, or making up a shopping list, they will feel that they can do this too.

Experiences and resources to support mark making

The following extract is taken from Mark Making (National Strategies).

The following suggested experiences and resources will support practitioners in making sure that a good range of mark-making experiences, tools and resources are available, both as part of continuous provision and as provocations for new thinking.

Inside experiences:

- *Registers – self-registration marks*

- *Name writing – different purposes*

- *Diaries and calendars – recording significant events*

- *Telephone/address book – recording phone numbers and addresses*

- *Cooking – writing recipes and ingredients, providing scales, clocks and timers to record weight, volume and time*

- *Dance – making marks to music, ribbons on sticks*

- *Office – taking messages, signing in or out*

- *Art area – collages, painting, gluing, using clay*

- *Quiet area – pads, paper and pens to record feelings*

- *Graphics area – different types of paper, letters, envelopes and stamps, postcards, tickets, maps, plus opportunities for recording counting, measuring and quantities*

- *Recording measurements in big block area*

book of words that you are introducing the children to. In this way, children will make links with the sounds and the letters. If children are to make sense of the meaning of the words, they can be put into sentences, for example:

Today, we opened a box and inside the box we found a cup, a car, a spoon and a peg.

As children move on, they can be introduced to more complicated sounds within words, such as b-oa -t and to gain an understanding about vowels and consonants.

In terms of **writing**, let's look at how you can:

1. Enable children to use their phonic knowledge to write words in ways which match their spoken sounds.

2. Provide children with opportunities to write some irregular common words.

3. Support children to write simple sentences which can be read by themselves and others.

- *Music area – recording the beat, length of sounds*

- *White boards in group areas – registration, names, recording counting and calculations*

- *Role-play area, e.g. shoe shop – filling in slips and order forms, shoe sizes on boxes*

- *Small world area – drawing maps, roads, homes, directions.*

Outside experiences:

- *Big chalks on floor*

- *Mud and twigs of different lengths and sizes*

- *Sensory play – making marks on builders trays in different textures*

- *Playhouse with pads, paper, books*

- *Gazebo – clipboards and paper, envelopes*

- *Fabric sheets – with mud, sticks different lengths and widths*

- *Maps – huge sheets, fat felt pens*

- *Spray painting – water sprayers*

- *Picnic table covered in large sheets of paper*

- *Rolls of paper on the floor*

- *Mark-making trolley – variety of equipment, different shapes and sizes*

- *Forest area, making marks with sticks in the mud*

- *Garage area, filling in slips, recording findings.*

Think about the broader picture too – developing children's awareness of other languages and writing systems other than English.

Remember that there are other ways of communicating, such as Braille, for the visually impaired.

Consider doing things on a big scale, rather than just providing standard sized paper – use rolls of wall paper which can be attached to tables or spread out on the floor.

Whatever attempts the children make in their 'writing' remember that these early lines/squiggles are meaningful to the child, and they show that the child is beginning to understand writing.

In terms of letter recognition, use large foam letters, magnetic letters, display an alphabet frieze, or perhaps even make your own with the children. Avoid rushing the reading and writing process – these skills develop over a long period. Remember that children need to learn how to hold a pencil/crayon/chalk stick. It is all about co-ordination and plenty of time to practice in a fun way, without placing pressure on the children. To support the children's co-ordination, think about ways in which you can develop their whole body, and also their hand and finger play skills. Large movements, such as throwing and catching balls contribute to the co-ordination

children need for their handwriting skills. In terms of smaller movements, action rhymes which involve the child in moving hands and fingers, for example, incy wincy spider, will help them make co-ordinated moves. Other tasks such as washing dolls clothes and pegging them on the line is fun.

Avoid placing pens, crayons etc. in the child's hands – let them use the hand that feel most natural to them, and then guide them to how they may best grip the writing tool. Think about ways in which you can do writing together with the children, such as by making shopping lists (perhaps with drawings too). A fun idea is for the adult to write very simple messages for a small group of children as part of a game to find something in the setting – hide a specific toy that all the children would recognise, and show a picture of the toy.

Hold up word cards that guide the children on where to look first – use symbols such as arrow marks as well as words to help them. Allow the children to look in a few places before 'finding' the toy.

Mathematics

This is about providing children with opportunities to develop and improve their skills in counting, understanding and using numbers, calculating simple addition and subtraction problems and to describe shapes, spaces, and measures.

Early Learning Goals

Numbers

Children count reliably with numbers from 1 to 20, place them in order and say which number is one more or one less than a given number. Using quantities and objects, they add and subtract two single-digit numbers and count on or back to find the answer. They solve problems, including doubling, halving and sharing.

Shape, space and measures

Children use everyday language to talk about size, weight, capacity, position, distance, time and money to compare quantities and objects and to solve problems. They recognise, create and describe patterns. They explore characteristics of everyday objects and shapes and use mathematical language to describe them.

In terms of **numbers**, let's look at how you can:

1. Provide children with opportunities to count using numbers from 1-20.

2. Support children to add and subtract two single-digit numbers and count on or back to find the answer.

3. Enable children to solve problems, including doubling, halving and sharing.

Staff at Victoria Park Nursery School encourage the children to count in a wide variety of ways to stimulate their interests in numbers. From solving practical problems such as, 'how many biscuits do we need?' to counting balls in the outdoor area as they are being put away, staff make use of any opportunity within the session to develop this area of learning for each child. Number rhymes are popular and are frequently included in song time. Rhymes such as Five Little Ducks, do not actually teach the children the meaning of the numbers, but do give children helpful reminders about their order.

'Numbers' need to be made real for children. When someone says 'she really knows her numbers' they are likely to mean that she can recite the names of the numbers in ascending order. What matters is how children understand what numbers are and how they relate to one another.

Think about numbers that can be 'seen', such as 3 cars, 3 bricks, 3 dolls etc. These numbers are real and can be seen, counted up and counted back down again. When we think about numbers that cannot be seen, such as 3 years old, we are not helping children with the concept of number. Children need to be able to see and handle objects – they can check that the count is right, and can understand that to remove one object from three will leave two remaining. When children count what they can see, they begin to understand that counting involves each object being matched with a single number.

The best way to approach counting is naturally through play. Staff at Victoria Park Nursery School encourage children to count in the home corner when they are working out how many plates are needed for the people sitting around the table. Children come to understand the concept of rationing – as a limited number of aprons are made available for activities such as painting or water play, so children start to recognise that there is one apron per child. This is quite a complex concept, however, children are helped by staff who are sensitive to each child's stage of development.

Remember that numbers can also be represented by symbols. Marks, such as short straight lines, pictures, dots, the number itself, and by the spoken word are examples that can be used in a variety of ways.

Snack time provides staff with opportunities to help children with an understanding of whole, halves, quarters etc. and to use maths language to represent shapes, sizes and weight. When children share something between two, they begin to understand that they have a half each, two halves make a whole and so on...

Children love problems! It is a sad fact that, for so many adults, maths is associated with failure – a problem for them. "I can't do maths" is often said by those who did not have a positive experience of maths at school. If children pick up on these messages, the negative message may become a view of the child too, so maths needs to be approached in a fun way that makes problem solving interesting, challenging, but also achievable for the child.

Let's look at some links between play and maths:

- In terms of creative play (water, sand, dough, paint and junk modelling), children can explore shape, weight, capacity and volume.

- In terms of board games (puzzles, card games, dominoes), children can follow instructions, use sequencing, count up and down, explore differences, fit things together without leaving any spaces.

- Children cannot always work things out by themselves. The role of the adult is to support learning by prompting children and asking questions, such as:

  ○ How many have we got altogether?

  ○ How many would we have if I took one away?

  ○ How many do we need?

  ○ How can we make sure that everyone can have some apple?

  ○ How shall we solve the problem?

In terms of **shape, space and measures**, let's look at how you can:

1. Encourage children to use everyday language to talk about size, weight, capacity, position, distance, time and money to compare quantities and objects and to solve problems.

2. Provide children with opportunities to recognise, create and describe patterns.

3. Support children to explore everyday objects and shapes and use mathematical language to describe them.

Staff at Victoria Park Nursery School encourage the children's use of mathematical language in all aspects of their play.

1. At the water and sand tray.

2. Specific role play activities such as a shop to encourage talk around money.

3. Cooking provides lots of opportunities for discussion about weight, size and capacity.

4. Day routines encourage the beginnings of discussion about time, tidy up time, lunch time, home time.

5. Looking at a clock, children will start to understand that 'when the big hand gets to number 12 it is time to go'.

6. Sand timers show visually when it is time to give the toy to the next person.

7. In the outdoor area positional language can be used –'you are at the top of the ladder', 'crawl through the barrel'.

8. Small world play – 'the duck is behind the cow'.

9. Children lining up – 'Nathan is in front of Ashraf'.

10. Measuring – have a measuring tape tacky backed to a unit top where children can use it.

11. Patterning with natural objects in the garden – fir cones, pebbles, shells, conkers, twigs.

12. Patterning with bottle tops.

13. Looking at patterns on clothes – 'who is wearing stripes?' 'Is anyone wearing spots?'.

14. Diwali patterns.

15. Tangrams – this is a sort of puzzle, something created by splitting up a shape into pieces. Divide a square cardboard shape into smaller shapes and ask children to recreate the square from the smaller shapes.

16. Looking for shapes in the environment and setting up trails.

There are various ways children can be helped with to develop their mathematical understanding. When you ask a child or a group of children questions such as:

- Who came first, second and third in the race?

- How many more do we need?

- What comes before number 8?

- What comes after number 3?

- Are there enough coins?

- Which container holds the most/less water?

You are giving them an opportunity to think about what they are doing in the activity, and what the outcome could be. Make maths games fun as well as for a purpose – for example, provide a washing line with a set number of pegs to hang out pairs of socks – will you offer more or less pegs than are needed to hang out the socks? The children will enjoy sorting the socks into pairs, and then working out how many pegs they will need. Number some containers and ask the children to find, for example, 8 buttons to put in the container with the number 8 written on it. A variation of this could be to hang pockets, with numbers on each pocket, on a wall that the children can access. Remember that all maths games/activities will need you to engage with the children- you are helping them to develop their maths language.

A fun idea for outside is to find, for example, 5 green items and bring them in for a number 5 table – the children may find a blade of grass, a leaf or a toy from the garden. Another idea is a 'number walk', when the children need to look for the number 6, for example, as they walk around – this could be in shop window, the library, on a car number plate etc. Of course, it is also important for the children to have opportunities to write numbers – they can have fun 'writing' numbers in foam or paint, even writing in the air! A fun game could be to float foam numbers in the water play tray and see if the children can lift them out in the correct numerical order. Make a chart to show what scores everyone achieves.

Children can make junk models with different sized cartons and boxes and add other materials. Provide the materials, pens/paint, sticky tape and scissors, and allow the children to make their own model. These can be displayed for all to enjoy.

Understanding the world

This is about guiding children to make sense of their physical world and their community through opportunities to explore, observe and find out about people, places, technology and the environment.

Early Learning Goals

People and communities
Children talk about past and present events in their own lives and in the lives of family members. They know that other children don't always enjoy the same things, and are sensitive to this. They know about similarities and differences between themselves and others, and among families, communities and traditions.

The World
Children know about similarities and differences in relation to places, objects, materials and living things. They talk about the features of their own immediate environment and how environments might vary from one another. They make observations of animals and plants and explain why some things occur, and talk about changes.

Technology
Children recognise that a range of technology is used in places such as homes and schools. They select and use technology for particular purposes.

In terms of **people and communities**, let's look at how you can:

1. Provide children with opportunities to talk about past and present events in their own lives and in the lives of family members.

2. Support children to understand that other children don't always enjoy the same things, and are sensitive to this.

3. Encourage children to explore similarities and differences between themselves and others, and among families, communities and traditions.

Staff at The Village Montessori Nursery School support children to make sense of their physical world in a wide variety of ways. Children are introduced to people of the world when they learn about our planet and its continents. Staff provide children with pictures of families from different continents along with artefact boxes including objects which represent lifestyles and animals on the different continents.

Children are introduced to celebrations and festivals of people from various faiths and communities as well as exploring food, music, dancing and clothing from different countries. Each child is encouraged to respect diversity of cultures whilst recognising similarities and acknowledging shared needs by being encouraged to think of themselves as 'Citizens of the World'. This exploration usually begins with the children looking at themselves and their own families.

When we work with children, we have a responsibility to help them to recognise the individuality of others, and to value differences between individuals and groups

In terms of **the world**, let's look at how you can:

1. Broadly support children to know about similarities and differences in relation to places, objects, materials and living things.

2. Enable children to talk about the features of their own immediate environment and how environments might vary from one another.

3. Provide children with opportunities to make observations of animals and plants and explain why some things occur, and talk about changes.

The Village Montessori Nursery School supports children to learn about the physical features of the world by exploring, through the use of Montessori resources, the solar system, the structure of the Earth, volcanoes, the Earth and it's physical features, that is, land, water, air, mountains, rivers, deserts, rainforests, islands, lakes etc. Within the setting, children become familiar with the natural features of the immediate environment by exploring the garden area and nearby fields, woodland areas and stream – this is where the children learn to identify seasonal changes, familiar trees and animals. Children also have opportunities to observe natural features of the environment by observing, investigating and looking after the vegetable and herb gardens, the orchard area, and the stick insects and farm animals in the adjoining fields. Children bring their experiences from the outdoor classroom to the indoor areas to explore them further, for example, life cycle models – the butterfly life cycle (with actual caterpillars) – the frog life cycle. Children pair objects with pictures of plants, fruit and vegetable and animals. Classification and Terminology cards are used to support the children's understanding of animals of the world/continent/country. Children are also encouraged to take responsibility for maintaining and caring for their immediate environments and participate in recycling projects.

If children are to make sense of the world about them, they need to be provided with opportunities to observe and investigate the natural environment. Provide tools such as microscopes, to enable children to look closely at the small animal and plant world. This will develop their curiosity, and allow them to look at similarities and differences. It is important to give children time to explore and describe what they have found and to be able

in our society. When children are involved in their local communities, they begin to appreciate and respect the way other people lead their day to day lives. Inviting members of the community into the setting gives children an insight into how the community works together for the benefit of all. Children and their families should be comfortable about their own identity and feel free of prejudice or any kind of discrimination.

When choices in play are made available to children, they begin to recognise what their own interests are and that other children may have different interests to theirs. When children are involved and able to make choices, their learning is more meaningful.

Staff of the Village Montessori Nursery School engage with children as they explore pictorial timelines, such as their own day of the week at nursery or their life from birth to the present. Older children in the nursery explore stories of the animal and plant kingdom by the use of the pre-historic timeline. Montessori materials and resources are provided to help the children work towards the early learning goals.

to ask questions. The adult needs to be involved and interested in each child's discovery, working from each child's interests and helping them to develop appropriate vocabulary in connection with their findings. Let children help you devise ways to record findings.

Allow children to spend time sorting, matching, classifying and comparing things. Children are naturally interested in investigating – work together with the children to develop their investigational skills. Encourage them to look for patterns and connections in what they have found – all these things help children to make sense of the world about them. Give children opportunities to predict what might happen and make judgements

Above all, make this area of learning fun! Involve the children in making decisions about what they would like to do, how they can share what they have found with others and how they can record their findings.

In terms of **technology**, let's look at how you can:

1. Support children to recognise that a range of technology is used in places such as homes and schools.

2. Provide children with opportunities to select and use technology for particular purposes.

The Village Montessori Nursery School introduces and encourages children to use appropriate technology – this includes cameras, microscopes and the computer. Children are also shown how to safely use a range of relevant utensils and tools when cooking, gardening, sewing and when engaged in simple carpentry. ICT equipment is only introduced to the children once they have a good grasp of their environment, as they are encouraged to explore, investigate and learn about the environment from real experiences.

For many settings, ICT conjures up thoughts of the computer; however, ICT is much broader than the use of a computer! ICT is about in the everyday world and things that are used daily by us all – vacuum cleaners, microwave ovens, DVD players/recorders, digital cameras, photocopiers etc. As adults, we take all these for granted, but for children, ICT needs to be available in the setting to help them make sense of how these things impact on our lives. What you provide will enable children

to explore technology in a safe environment. Remove the back off a radio, leave it on a table, and you will see how many children come over to see what this is all about! ICT is strong when staff interact with the children, sharing in their interest, observing them and then planning to develop the interest noted. When children develop a new ICT skill, encourage them to share this knowledge with other children. Of course, not all staff may feel confident about the use of ICT themselves, so this could become real opportunity for everyone to learn together. Computer games are becoming very popular, and whilst they are fun and have elements of learning, it is worth balancing these games with discovery sites to further inspire the children.

The home corner is a rich environment for ICT learning – the telephone, cooker, kettle, iron, clock, radio, TV with remote control – and anything that has a dial for the children to use.

The home corner could become a bank – add a computer, telephone, photocopier, cash machine, till, calculator, fax machine alongside paper and pens.

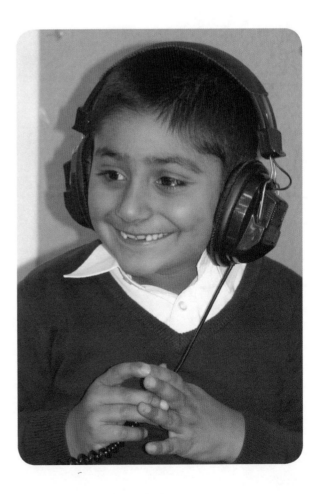

The home corner could also become a photo gallery of the children's own photos – the children could make numbered tickets for people visiting the gallery. The children could design the display area for the photographs to be shown – perhaps based on a theme, such as 'what we like doing in our nursery' or 'this is me'!

Photos of what the children have done during the session could be made into a slide show for parents to see as they collect their children.

Children love projects – they could be encouraged to take photographs as the project moves forward, showing the progress.

A good fun game – let the children take photographs of everyday items from an unusual angle or just a small part of the items and then let others guess what the item could be.

ICT can be fun – from programmable toys to drills, telephones to cameras, calculators to computers, develop your resources to cover all areas of learning.

Expressive arts and design

This is about enabling children to explore and play with a wide range of media and materials, as well as providing opportunities and encouragement for sharing their thoughts, ideas and feelings through a variety of activities in art, music, movement, dance, role-play and design and technology.

Early Learning Goals

Exploring and using media and materials

Children sing songs, make music and dance, and experiment with ways of changing them. They safely use and explore a variety of materials, tools and techniques, experimenting with colour, design, texture, form and function.

Being imaginative

Children use what they have learnt about media and materials in original ways, thinking of their uses and purposes. They represent their own ideas, thoughts and feelings through design and technology, art, music, dance, role-play and stories.

In terms of **exploring and using media and materials**, let's look at ways in which you can:

1. Encourage children to sing songs, make music and dance, and experiment with ways of changing them.

2. Provide children with a variety of materials, tools and techniques, experimenting with colour, design, texture, form and function.

The Village Montessori Nursery School ensures that children have access to high quality resources which will develop the skills that are essential for children to engage in spontaneous creative activities. In practice, this means children are learning how to:

1. Use scissors and glue

2. Use different types of paint with large and small brushes

3. Printing

4. Make a collage using a variety of materials such as paper, textiles and natural materials

5. Use stencils

6. Create with playdough

7. Make models with clay

8. Use other modelling materials

9. Make three dimensional constructions from a variety of materials – paper, cardboard, wood and construction wooden blocks.

In addition, children have daily opportunities to sing and use the musical instruments.

In your setting, think about ways in which children can be provided with opportunities to describe the texture of things. Record children's responses to different textures, for example, touching sections of a texture display with their fingers, or feeling it with their cheeks to get a sense of different properties.

Make time and space for children to express their curiosity and explore the environment using all of their senses. Introduce vocabulary to enable children to talk about their observations and experiences, for example, 'smooth', 'shiny', 'rough', 'prickly', 'flat', 'patterned', 'jagged', 'bumpy', 'soft' and 'hard'.

Think about ways in which colour can be explored, taking into account children's growing interest in and use of colour as they begin to find differences between colours. Talk to a child about images or effects that they see, such as the effect of light hitting a shiny piece of paper. Provide a wide range of materials, resources and sensory experiences to enable children to explore colour, texture and space.

Document the processes children go through to create their own 'work'. One child may spontaneously make lots of 'spiral' marks and movements on their paper, while others may imitate each other's movements. Talk to children about colours they like and why they like them. Provide a place where work in progress can be kept safely. Talk to children about where they can see models and plans in the environment, such as at the local planning office, in the town square, or at the new apartments down the road.

Think about how children may use their bodies to explore texture and space. Demonstrate and teach skills and techniques associated with the things children are doing, for example, show them how to stop the paint from dripping or how to balance bricks so that they will not fall down.

Think about the patterns and structures children talk about, make or construct. Introduce children to a wide range of music, painting and sculpture.

Establish which songs are most popular and encourage all of the children to join in – if they have made instruments, these can be used to accompany the songs. Children can be encouraged to be interested in music and sounds from birth.

After joining in with a few familiar songs, children can move on to songs that are new to them with some confidence. Encourage the children to tap their feet to repeated rhythms for an additional experience. Musical activities will help children learn about different melodies, rhythm and beat, timings and also the sequence of the sounds.

Some practitioners believe that they need to be musical themselves to be able to provide musical activities for the children. This is not the case – the main idea is to make sounds and music fun – making sounds with instruments, regardless of how they sound, is the way in which children start to explore sound and the effects of sounds. Value what the children do – be led by them and use music tapes if you are unsure of your ability to sing well. This shows confidence to the children you are working with. Keep music times within the session special – they are a key part of the day when children can come together and have fun as they make sounds to music, make up their own songs and foster their own imagination. If you know of any musicians in your local community, consider inviting them in to work with the children to gain a different perspective.

In terms of **being imaginative**, let's look at how you can:

1. Support children to think about what they use, and what they have learnt about media and materials.

2. Provide opportunities for children to represent their own ideas, thoughts and feelings through design and technology, art, music, dance, role-play and stories.

Staff of The Village Montessori Nursery School encourage children to express their ideas spontaneously using a variety of media and through words, music, movement and dance as well as stories. Children have opportunities to express their ideas through spontaneous role play and they are encouraged to explore the possibilities regarding resources for role play and its focus. Staff are enthusiastic, supportive, sensitive and encouraging. They explore the possible use of resources and discuss how best to achieve the child's desired outcomes. Staff do not lead the creative process as this tends to limit the opportunities for the children to express themselves spontaneously.

Music can be soothing, at times of the day when the children need to calm down, or can be a stimulant. Provide a range of musical activities for the children that could include a variety of tempos (pace or speed) such as loud, soothing, quick etc.

Think about how you can encourage co-operation and communication with the children during role play and as they engage in movement, dance and musical activities. Allow time for children to express themselves as they explore and investigate things they come across. Repetition is crucial to consolidate learning – repeat activities often in order to build the children's confidence and let them practise new skills.

Think about the benefits of musical expression for children who have learning difficulties. Repetition of sounds within songs enables children with opportunities to practise sounds over and over again. Language, when incorporated into songs and rhymes, is easier to learn.

Children who find it hard to concentrate may benefit when they have opportunities for real active participation in a wide range of enjoyable activities, including musical expression.

Providing well planned opportunities for children to express themselves through art, music and role play has benefits for all children. Role play allows children to learn about other cultures, it encourages individual as well as small group co-operative play, can help children to learn to empathise with others as well as making sense of the world around them.

Make sure that you take role play outside and not just think about opportunities for indoor role play. Look at your resources to ensure that you can rotate to maintain interest – include opportunities for children to write as well as providing IT choices.

Think about using a variety of different tools or materials to make different sounds, such as metal spoons, wood, leaves etc. Make a sound wall – let the children find things from outside or inside that they can make different noises with, to attach to the wall. A sound bag provides fun and encourages the children to listen and concentrate. Let the children know that you have placed a number of things in a bag that all make a sound. Put your hand in the bag, but without the children seeing what you are doing, and make a noise with one thing you have placed in the bag. Can the children guess what is making the noise? Can they describe the noise?

Use books to stimulate children's interest and imagination. Change your voice to become, for example, a pirate, as you read the story. Let the children act out a favourite story by dressing up, making sounds with instruments and changing their voices to become characters in the story. Encourage children to make up their own stories, and draw the pictures to go with them.

Section Three:
The Early Years
Foundation Stage Profile

In 2013, the Standards and Testing Agency produced the EYFS Profile Handbook. Exemplifications materials to support the handbook have also been produced. Alongside these two documents, the Assessment and Reporting Arrangements (ARA) have also been made available.

There is an expectation that the Handbook, ARA and Exemplification materials will be used by Local Authorities, Head teachers and Early Years Professionals, as the documents contain the information needed about the assessment of children's attainment. Crucially for the practitioner, there is guidance on making accurate and reliable judgements about EYFS attainment.

So, what does this mean for you?

Before we explore the details of the Profile, we need to consider the earlier assessment within the EYFS: the **Progress Check for Two-Year-Olds**.

The Progress Check is explained clearly in the 'Know How' guidance document, which was produced by the National Children's Bureau. It makes clear that the progress check:

1. should be completed by a practitioner who knows the child well and works directly with them in the setting. This should normally be the child's key person;

2. arises from the ongoing observational assessments carried out as part of everyday practice in the setting;

2. you ensure that parents have a clear picture of their child's development;

3. the check enables practitioners to understand the child's needs and plan activities to meet them in the setting;

4. the check enables parents to understand the child's needs and, with support from practitioners, enhance development at home;

5. you note areas where a child is progressing well and identify any areas where progress is less than expected; and

6. you describe actions you intend to take to address any developmental concerns (including working with other professionals where appropriate).

Strong emphasis is placed on the role of parents in connection with the Progress Check. The Know How guidance document makes clear that:

'A starting point for all assessment should be an acknowledgement that parents know their children best. They are their child's first and most enduring educators, with in-depth knowledge of their child's physical, emotional and language development over time. This knowledge should be reflected in both on-going dialogue and in the progress check'.

Parents and practitioners should reflect together on what:

1. a child likes to do;

2. he/she is trying to master or has just learned;

3. new words/language structures are emerging; and

4. particular interests or patterns in play and exploration are observed at the moment.

The Know How guide also makes clear that, in order for the child to be supported in his/her learning:

'Parents and practitioners use this shared knowledge and understanding in order to plan together and think through ideas of how to move the child forward. Learning

3. is based on skills, knowledge, understanding and behaviour that the child demonstrates consistently and independently;

4. takes account of the views and contributions of parents;

5. takes into account the views of other practitioners and, where relevant, other professionals working with the child;

6. enables children to contribute actively to the process.

Why has this check been introduced? A midway check within the EYFS to see how a child is developing will assist you in determining how best to support the child leading up to the end of the EYFS.

The 'Know How' aims are clear:

1. you review a child's development in the three prime areas of the EYFS;

opportunities and next steps can be planned for the setting and the home. This process builds on what parents know and do already with their child, and supports their confidence and knowledge in how to extend and strengthen the early home learning environment. The most useful and valuable summaries will be clear and easy to read, be easy to understand, avoiding unfamiliar jargon, present a truthful, yet sensitive, reflection of what the child can do and their achievements to date, identify areas where the child is progressing at a slower pace than expected, recognise parents' in-depth knowledge of their child by incorporating their observations and comments, give parents an idea of how their child's development will be taken forward in the setting, provide some suggestions for parents in supporting their child at home and reflect their child's individual personality and characteristics'.

So, it is important that you understand what is meant by Communication and Language, Physical Development and Personal, Emotional and Social Development as these three represent the Prime Areas of Learning. Again, broadly:

Communication and Language

This is all about developing children's listening and attention skills, helping children's understanding of language and developing their speaking skills.

Physical Development

This is all about helping children to be able to move around and be able to handle things. It is also about helping children to understand about health and their own self-care.

Personal, Social and Emotional development

This is all about developing children's self-confidence and self-esteem, that is – how children feel about themselves. It is also about helping children to manage their feelings and their behaviour, and supporting children to make relationships with others and to understand others too.

It is also important that you understand what is meant by the Characteristics of Effective Learning. When you observe children, you are recording not only what you have seen, but HOW that learning showed. The Characteristics of Effective Learning are:

- **playing and exploring** – children investigate, experience things and are willing to 'have a go';

- **active learning** – children concentrate and keep on trying if they encounter difficulties and enjoy achievements; and

- **creating and thinking critically** – children have and develop their own ideas, make links between ideas and develop strategies for doing things.

When a child is between the age of two and three years, you need to complete a short written report on the child's development, this is the Progress Check. In the back of the Know How guidance, you will find examples of how you can make your record of the child's development. These examples are for you to consider – you may use them or devise your own. The main point is that you include the development in the Prime Areas as well as comments on the way in which the child is currently learning.

Statutory Framework

At the end of the EYFS – that is, 'in the final term of the year in which the child reaches age five, and no later

than 30 June in that term, the EYFS Profile must be completed for each child. The Profile provides parents and carers, practitioners and teachers with a well-rounded picture of a child's knowledge, understanding and abilities, their progress against expected levels, and their readiness for Year 1. The Profile must reflect: ongoing observation; all relevant records held by the setting; discussions with parents and carers, and any other adults whom the teacher, parent or carer judges can offer a useful contribution. Each child's level of development must be assessed against the early learning goals. Practitioners must indicate whether children are meeting expected levels of development, if they are exceeding expected levels, or not yet reaching expected levels ('emerging'). This is the EYFS Profile'.

In *The Early Years: Foundations for life, health and learning* (An Independent Report on the Early Years Foundation Stage) Dame Clare Tickell says:

> '*Throughout the review, I have heard mixed and strong views on the topic of assessment at the end*

of the EYFS – the EYFS Profile. On balance, the majority agree we should retain a summative, or summary, assessment at the end of the reception year, but it is also clear that the existing EYFS Profile is too detailed and complex. More could be done to maximise the value of the information, particularly to Year 1 teachers. Many have spoken to me about the burdens they feel have been introduced by this assessment, through paperwork and through moderation and inspection processes. There are strong arguments for retaining summative assessment at the end of the EYFS. An improved framework for assessment at the end of the EYFS would ensure consistency of practice between different settings, and therefore consistency of experience for children – in terms of the support they receive while in early years settings, and the information shared with parents and carers to help them understand how their child is doing. If successful, it should also help to make the transition between the early years and Key Stage 1 as smooth and effective as possible*'.

So, what does the 2013 Profile looks like?

Refer to the Handbook, which covers:

1. Introduction

2. EYFS Profile purposes, principles and processes

3. Inclusion

4. Completing the EYFS Profile

5. Exemplification of expected descriptors

6. Moderation of the EYFS Profile

7. Quality assurance of the EYFS Profile.

Let's focus on 5.3 – Areas and aspects of learning of the EYFS and their associated ELGs, as there are useful explanatory notes alongside each early learning goal. IMPORTANT NOTE: The purpose of the brief explanatory note is to provide a concise explanation for each ELG to ensure accuracy and consistency of interpretation by all stakeholders.

The explanatory note is not to be used in place of the ELG descriptor as described in Sections One and Two of this book and in the Handbook, for assessment purposes.

Prime areas of learning

Communication and language

Early Learning Goal 01

Listening and attention

Explanatory note: *The child listens actively while engaged in a variety of activities from which he or she is able to recall significant details. This includes stories and rhymes. When listening to suggestions or explanations, the child responds appropriately through actions or comments, predicting what might happen or by asking relevant questions. The child remains focused on an activity, can sustain a conversation with someone as they play and perseveres despite distractions showing consistently high levels of involvement.*

Early Learning Goal 02

Understanding

Explanatory note: *The child is able to understand and respond to a series of simple steps in order to complete familiar or unfamiliar activity. The child is able to answer questions about their own activities or experiences and is able to demonstrate understanding by answering questions including 'how' and 'why' about stories and events.*

Early Learning Goal 03

Speaking

Explanatory note: *The child uses speech to recreate, rehearse and reflect on his or her experiences and to clarify ideas and feelings. The child is keen to develop their vocabulary and may demonstrate their understanding of newly learned words by using them in context. The child speaks clearly and with confidence in both familiar and less familiar groups. They demonstrate an awareness of the listener, for example by adding detail to explanations or asking questions in order to find out more information.*

2013 Early Years Foundation Stage Profile Handbook 25

Physical development

Early Learning Goal 04

Moving and handling

Explanatory note: *The child demonstrates coordination and control in both fine and gross motor activities. A range of equipment and tools are manipulated appropriately and confidently. The child shows an awareness of space, adjusting speed and direction purposefully and negotiating small and large spaces successfully and safely. The child competently produces marks with a range of mark making tools.*

Early Learning Goal 05

Health and self-care

Explanatory note: *The child shows some knowledge and understanding of the factors that contribute to keeping healthy, such as physical exercise and a balanced diet. They are able to express themselves about things they could do to keep themselves healthy and safe. The child shows personal independence by demonstrating healthy practices in their everyday life.*

2013 Early Years Foundation Stage Profile Handbook 26

Early Learning Goal 06

Self-confidence and self-awareness

Explanatory note: *The child makes choices within their environment and expresses their preferences. The child tries new things, explores resources and tools, and shares their experiences with others including adults, peers or within a group. The child plays independently expressing their ideas and innovations and asks for support when needed.*

Early Learning Goal 07

Managing feelings and behaviour

Explanatory note: *The child responds appropriately to experiences, communicating his or her needs, views and feelings. The child is aware of the consequences of words and actions and adapts his or her behaviour accordingly. When playing as part of a group, the child takes turns and shares. The child knows the expectations and routines of the setting, applies* strategies to respond to changes of routine and offers explanations as to why these are necessary. The child is usually able to adjust his or her behaviour to reflect this understanding.

Early Learning Goal 08

Making relationships

Explanatory note: *The child plays co-operatively in a group, sharing and taking turns. When playing together with others, the child usually responds in a friendly and kind way, listening to other children's ideas and points of view. The child interacts positively with other children and adults.*

Specific Areas of Learning

Literacy

Early Learning Goal 09

Reading

Explanatory note: *The child uses cues such as pictures, letter/word recognition, knowledge of the story or context and reading for meaning, in order to help them comprehend a range of fiction and non-fiction texts. The child blends and segments words independently and applies their phonic knowledge to regular and irregular unfamiliar words. The child shares his or her feelings and ideas about what they have read with others.*

Early Learning Goal 10

Writing

Explanatory note: *The child writes for a range of purposes in meaningful contexts. The child's writing may include features of different forms such as stories, lists, labels, captions, recipes, instructions and letters. The child's writing is phonetically plausible when he or she writes simple regular words and particularly when he or she attempts to write more complex words. The child and others can read and make sense of the text.*

2013 Early Years Foundation Stage Profile Handbook 28

Mathematics

Early Learning Goal 11

Numbers

Explanatory note: *Within play and other practical situations, the child counts and orders numbers from 1-20 and finds one more or one fewer than a given number. Using every day and play objects, the child applies a range of strategies to add and subtract quantities involving two single-digit numbers such as counting on to add and counting back to subtract. In a range of practical and play contexts the child explores and solves problems involving doubling, halving and sharing, utilising his or her own methods.*

Early Learning Goal 12

Shape, space and measures

Explanatory note: *The child uses everyday language to share their thinking about size, weight, capacity, position, distance, time and money. The child demonstrates that they understand that one quantity is different to another even if they do not know the correct comparative term. The child is able to recognise and describe patterns and notices them in the environment. The child makes patterns using a range of media and resources. The child notices and describes everyday objects and shapes using appropriate mathematical language.*

2013 Early Years Foundation Stage Profile Handbook 29

Understanding the world

Early Learning Goal 13

People and communities

Explanatory note: *The child communicates about events involving them and family members, now and in the past. They listen, comment and show sensitivity towards other children's experiences, communities and traditions which may be the same or different to their own. This may be demonstrated through their behaviour, actions or communications.*

Early Learning Goal 14

The world

Explanatory note: *The child has a curiosity and interest about the immediate environment around them and recognises when things have similar or different features. Whilst exploring through play and real experiences, the child shows their learning and understanding of living things, materials and objects. The child investigates, notices changes and interacts with elements of their natural and manufactured environment. He or she communicates about what is happening and why.*

Early Learning Goal 15

Technology

Explanatory note: *Through discussion, play and practical application the child demonstrates that he or she knows about technology and its use in his or her life and local environment. The child chooses the technological opportunities around him or herself as a tool to enhance and extend his or her learning.*

2013 Early Years Foundation Stage Profile Handbook 30

Expressive arts and design

Early Learning Goal 16

Exploring and using media and materials

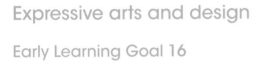

Explanatory note: *For the purpose of assessing this ELG: processes are more important than the finished product which need not necessarily occur; music is any generation of sound with intent to represent an idea or feeling; and dance is any form of movement by which children express themselves, emotions or responses. The child may recall and sing songs independently as he or she engages with other activities. The child creates and explores music and dance in their own way; they experiment and change sounds and movements in their play. The child uses a variety of materials, tools and techniques safely through an exploration of colour, design, texture, form and function.*

Early Learning Goal 17

Being imaginative

Explanatory note: *For the purpose of assessing this*

ELG: processes are more important than the finished product which need not necessarily occur; music is any generation of sound with intent to represent an idea or feeling; and dance is any form of movement by which children express themselves, emotions or responses. The child explores and experiments in a variety of imaginative ways in response to a range of creative stimuli. The child may use their prior knowledge and experience to express their ideas in original ways, making informed choices.

Dame Claire Tickell says:

'I am suggesting ways that the areas of development and early learning goals can be presented more simply and effectively. As part of this, the approach to assessment should be compatible with, and valuable to, primary school teachers so that a child's transition into Key Stage 1 is managed effectively and well. There are important opportunities here to recognise the value of reception as a transition year for children'.

In conclusion, this book has focused on the Early Learning Goals. Children will learn in an environment where they feel safe, loved and respected. The balance between nurture and structure is important for children – we must strive to provide a consistent approach to care and learning within the EYFS.

Nurture – this is about adults offering love and support so that children:

- feel loved and accepted

- receive warmth and affection

- are given time

- have their physical and emotional health protected and

- have their efforts praised.

Structure – this is about adults setting boundaries so that children:

- know the rules and what is expected of them, but that adults are flexible within these boundaries

- have space to express themselves and their opinions; and

- feel safe to try new things and make their own mistakes – and learn to be independent.

Dame Claire Tickell also made clear her views on supporting the move to Key Stage 1.

'*The first time that many children will experience the school environment is in reception class. I am clear that reception class should remain part of the EYFS – children in reception class are still very young, some only just 4-years-old, and there should continue to be a strong focus on supporting their development in the prime as well as the specific areas through play-based approaches. However, I think that children's experiences in reception class should help prepare them for the move to Year 1, both in terms of the level of development most children should have reached, and in the knowledge that most children would be expected to have. Skilled teachers and practitioners should be attuned to each child's level of development, to their pace of learning, and to their abilities and interests – and should determine the most effective approach to interacting with children to guide their development*'.

Acknowledgements

The author would like to sincerely thank the following settings for their time in contributing to this book. Each setting has focused on providing a wide variety of practical examples to assist practitioners in ways that they may support children throughout the EYFS.

Lynda Fright, EYFS Co-ordinator, John Rankin Infant and Nursery School, Newbury, West Berkshire.

Fiona Bridger Wilkinson, Headteacher, Victoria Park Nursery School, Newbury, West Berkshire.

Jackie Maclean, Headteacher, The Village Montessori Nursery School, Bradfield, West Berkshire.

Notes